SEVEN DECADES IN VERYAN

FRANK SYMONS

Seven Decades in Veryan

© Frank Symons

Cover photograph: ©Angelicia

First Edition published 2011

Published by:
Palores Publications,
11a Penryn Street, Redruth, Kernow TR15 2SP, UK.

Designed & Printed by:
The St Ives Printing & Publishing Company,
High Street, St Ives, Cornwall TR26 1RS, UK.

ISBN 978-1-906845-25-4

SEVEN DECADES
IN
VERYAN

FRANK SYMONS

ACKNOWLEDGMENT

The author would like to express his thanks to the publisher and printers and all those that have helped in any way, especially Mr Donald R. Rawe, who helped me get into publishing.

INTRODUCTION

Having lived so many years here in Veryan I've seen many changes. In the following pages I hope to include as many of these as possible. Some dates will be correct, others approximate. This is really a tale of the changing face of a village over seventy years. I will be concentrating mainly on the village and won't be able to include them all. To do so would make the end product far too expensive.

I have a vague memory of being in a field of hay, the crop lay in drams (swathes of cut hay) across the field and mum was turning it with a pike (two pronged fork) – that was during the summer of 1939.

My real memories though begin the following year . . .

Chapter One

THE 1940S

IN the spring of 1940 my aunty Hilda (mum's sister) died, and I recall going to her house and looking over the wall into a farmyard. There were masses of stocks in flower and a dear old dog named Sheppy. I don't recall going to that house again.

A few weeks later the billeting officer came to our door and asked could mum take some evacuees. Mum wasn't keen, saying she had just lost her sister. The officers reply was they would help her get over the loss. And so it was, in the middle of June, Beryl and Evelyn arrived from London. For nearly two years they enriched our household and became like sisters to me. When they went, so Beryl could attend a commercial college back home, we had another little girl for a time. As I have written a great deal concerning evacuees in previous books it would be repeating myself to say more.

During the period they were in Veryan and beyond, many homes had fathers, sons and daughters away serving their country. There were many service personnel in this area, at the Nare Hotel, Broom Park and Portloe. I well remember the American convoys rumbling through the village.

I also recall dad being in the Home Guard and still have his First Aid book today. Two of dad's brothers were in the army; one drove a tank the other was in the Military Police.

The men who weren't called up, many of whom worked long hours on the land, grew vegetables to feed their families – in some cases the families were very large. Most people had a garden, in fact there were twenty-six vegetable gardens here at Veryan Green. Many of these were at the allotment which ran down behind the blocks of houses below the famous round houses. During the planting season there would, of an evening, be eight or more men working there. It was where myself and some other boys were introduced to the soil. Men who hadn't joined up were members of the aforementioned Home Guard, the Fire Service or Observer Corps. At the start of war we even had Air Raid Wardens.

Those working on the land did a lot of overtime during hay and corn harvest, so the reader can see they had little spare time.

As stated farming was the main employer of labour, mainly men, helped admirably by girls who had joined the Land Army. Housewives helped with casual labour during potato planting and picking. Children over twelve were allowed time off school to help also. Mainly horses did the work, though there were a few Fordson tractors about. Towards the decades end people began looking further afield for employment. Men went to work in the clay industry near St Austell and girls, on leaving school, started moving away from domestic work.

Everyone worked from the age of 14 later 15; with big families parents were glad of any money they could earn. Boys were sent out with a pair of horses, to work the land. I know of one who says he was head horseman at fifteen. The corn harvest could last for weeks then as it did in the wet year of 1946. There were tractors but most farms still kept a horse to carry food out to their livestock. Bullocks for fattening were kept tied up indoors being let out only to drink while their stalls were cleared of droppings and hay or mangolds (turnips) put ready for them to eat. Sheep had their lambs in the fields which meant their owners being out in all weather and unsocial hours. In the early forties I recall watching my dad ploughing with two horses. He would arrive home tired after a day walking behind them.

Towards the close of that decade I recall the first cages in which laying hens were kept. I didn't like this method; I thought it cruel. Wages weren't high, about £3 per week on a farm. On leaving school a girl would earn about ten shillings a week doing housework. If she joined the Land Army at eighteen her wage would be over £2, out of which she had to pay the farmer for her keep. My parents had nearly six acres of land, five where we lived along with a meadow at Trewartha. It was less than half a mile away and I remember mum and I taking the cows up there. We walked them along the road which was quite safe then as there were few cars. About four hours later we would go and fetch them back as the land had no water.

The woman of the house worked just as hard, scrubbing floors, washing clothes by hand, picking wood and carrying all the households' water in buckets. She knitted garments for the family, made clothes, salted down the pig, which many homes fattened and killed, and even dug pits in the garden in which to tip the bucket from the outdoor toilet.

8

She cooked using a Cornish Range which couldn't be controlled, and did her mending by candlelight.

Children got to school as best they could for their mothers had no time to accompany them. Washing took one day, fetching wood and water for the job, much of another. By the mid forties washing was slightly easier as a few homes had electricity, and with it an electric boiler which took the place of the copper boiler. An electric kettle and iron helped a lot too. However it was well into the fifties before everyone in the village had these luxuries.

The two villages had only seventy-six dwellings between them. Thirty-seven in Veryan itself and thirty-nine further up at Veryan Green. Later in the decade two council houses were built at Veryan Green and the first tenants moving in just before Christmas 1944. Opposite these was what is now known as The Shambles, where Mrs Golbie lived. The plot of land below that house, which had been planted earlier to help the war effort, was now occupied by hens, ducks etc, owned by Mr Tregunna, one of the council house tenants. The six in Veryan were first occupied in the spring of 1948. But as two of the older ones had been knocked into one, the total was still only eighty-three houses. Apart from the taxis there were only three cars in each village, with two vans at the Green and three in Veryan itself.

Most homes had at least one bicycle, on which nearly everyone got to their job. A few even walking, in their case the many footpaths came in handy. For ordinary working folk the car was a luxury and there weren't many about in Veryan. We had two local bus owners; Mr Morse and Mr Tregunna, who went to Truro on Mondays, Wednesdays and Saturdays. The last two days we could even go to Truro of an evening to the cinema. They went to St Austell also on Tuesdays and Fridays, Mr Tregunna going through Port Holland. In 1947 Mr Morse moved from Treviskey to the new premises he'd had built near Cro-hans. The bus fare to Truro was two shillings and one could get a taxi for eighteen shillings. This same taxi would take one through *suicide alley* to the doctors for 20p or four shillings. A short distance from Mr Morse's new garage was a haulage business run by Mr Elliott, it dealt mainly with agriculture. Mr Palmer and his mate Jim Tregunna were blacksmiths at Bessie Beneath.

Veryan had two permanent butchers, Mr Elliott and Mr Webb while Miss Rundle and the Miss Bennetts were grocers. There was a cobbler, Mr Harris and Mr Phillips (who had only one arm) ran the pub. The post office (a little tiny place) was run jointly by Mr and Mrs Grose and what is now called Grannies Attic was rented by Mr Thomas, then Miss Deveral. Mr Reynolds who farmed Elerkey went to Portloe each Thursday selling fruit and vegetables on horse and wagon. A great many other people came round selling goods such as clothes, boots and shoes, mending wool and hardware. There were also two taxis driven by Mr Rawling, his son Stuart and Mr Tregunna, who was related to one of the bus owners. The policeman and nurse lived in the two houses behind the well at the top end of the school. During the forties three different policemen lived and worked in Veryan. Mr Howard (from whom dad bought our first wireless), Mr Mathews (whose wife ran the badminton club) and Mr Pankhurst. Just around the corner from them lived Mr Truscott who worked on a farm by day and cut men's hair of an evening in a wooden hut in the garden of Miss Dowrick's (Aunty Maud) house, with whom he, his wife and son lived.

I can recall two different men delivering our post, Mr Grose the postmaster and Mr Tucker. Mrs Grose helped in the office where they also handled the dole. It was very small, scarcely room to swing a cat, but they did good business. At one time Mr Grose took mail to Bessie Beneath on his bicycle where he passed it on to the mail van.

Though there was a good bus service to Truro and St Austell, people only went to buy things they couldn't get in Veryan. Many items were rationed and could only be obtained at the grocers where one was registered.

Medical care prior to the health service was costly. As already stated it meant hiring a taxi for the two mile journey to Trenance. On arrival one sat in a waiting room next to the surgery which was in a building close to the doctor's house. It was rare to find many people waiting as few could afford the fees. When mum took me to see him he would say, 'This boy needs a tonic.' Then off he would go into another room where he proceeded to wash out a bottle, fill it with water, add some colouring, and write something on the label, which couldn't be read. Our Doctor had a nurse, her name was Nurse Surley and she rode a bicycle in all weathers, even to deliver new born babies in the snow.

There was another doctor at St Mawes he also had one nurse. Dr Dyson sometimes helped out these two doctors. A dentist came to houses in Veryan of a Thursday afternoon for a while. I was nearly twelve years old when in July 1948 the National Health Service was brought into being by the then Labour Government. It was part of what was known as the Welfare State which would change people's lives. Dr Keith Scott joined his father here in 1947 and drove a sports car.

Mr Bennett, headmaster at the school, lived in what is now called The Old School House. He had been head since 1929. In 1940 he had to cope with an influx of children from London, then later from Bristol and Plymouth. In September that year I believe there were more evacuee children than locals. Extra classes were held in the British Legion Hall as it was then, and there were many London teachers – some of their names; Miss Colborne, Miss Sidney, Miss Thrower, Miss Henderson and Miss Gardner. Miss Thrower was officially a teacher at Ruan Lanihorne, but Miss Colborne and another teacher changed with her twice a week. That other teacher was Miss Walker, who taught me when I started school. Apart from those mentioned, there was a big turnover of staff that decade. Miss Colborne was here I think for three years, and her last day at school sticks in my memory. Mr Bennett got all us children into the middle room. It was packed as he paid her a warm tribute. We were quiet throughout his speech, but when he said "Three cheers for Miss Colborne" our cheers and stamping of feet nearly lifted the roof. The lady never taught me, but some she did teach said what a lot she brought to the school. I remember a few of the more local teachers, Miss Pascoe who lived locally and had taught at Veryan school for many years, was a tough case, tapping children on the head with a thimble when they misbehaved.

She was followed in the infants by Miss Craven, Miss Pearce and Miss Rawling. The junior's class also had changes; Mrs Bennett, Mrs Head, Mrs Williams, Miss Tallack, Mrs Greet and Miss Lloyd. When most of the evacuees had gone home there were 115 children. That state of affairs didn't last long and we soon had a second male teacher when first Mr Scofield then Mr Jordan arrived. The top two classes were split into three, the first for a short while and Mr Jordan only stayed about a year before Mr Taylor came. He rode a motor-cycle, which was kept in the boys' lobby. There were certainly more teachers, but those mentioned will do to be going on with. I think Mrs Williams was my teacher when school meals began. I was sitting with Peter Whetter in the front row, bang in front of the open fire, when on the first day we had stew. The plates, filled with stew, were put on our desks. But in a few weeks long tables soon arrived with forms for us to sit on. Mrs Moses was cook, assisted by Miss Johns and Miss Dowrick. The canteen provided meals for some 120 children and staff at the time. Its floor was given a thorough scrubbing every Friday afternoon. Mr Reynolds brought the milk, school children drunk during break time in buckets with lids.

In the late forties Mr Taylor was teaching one class the two same pieces of music for ages. We wondered why but soon found the answer when one afternoon, Bernard Fishwick from the BBC arrived. The two songs were recorded along with several local people for a programme presented every Sunday afternoon on the West of England Home Service. Bernard Fishwick was a short stocky man who wore a brown overcoat. The school doctor and a dentist would take over the infant's room now and again for a day or two and a man riding a bicycle came to tune the piano. Miss Pascoe finally retired but still came to teach the boys cane work for the autumn show. We had the Friday preceding it as a half term holiday. The spring half term was on Whitsun Monday. Late in the decade I was one of the gardening boys. About ten small plots were allotted to us boys while the girls planted flowers in borders just inside the gate. Half the area opposite the hall was so wet nothing could be planted in it. That end was near the water gardens where I recall moorhens lived on an island in the centre.

The autumn show took place on the first Saturday of November with exhibits in the school hall and playground. In the school there was industrial work, dairy produce, garden produce and children's exhibits. The boys' lobby was full of corn, while the yard was home to turnips, mangolds, cabbages, kale and hay. The hall was full of cages in which there were poultry, bantams, pigeons and rabbits. Mr Hearle was Hon. Secretary, followed by Mr F.G. Reynolds. There was a summer show for a few years. The hall had been built by men who came back from the first war, and was the venue for most of what went on in the village. Dances for the servicemen on Saturday nights, film shows on Monday evenings, a theatre company directed by Peter Alan which myself and a friend went to see 'The Corn is Green,' and an 'Any Questions' evening and several concerts. Women's Institute and British Legion parties for the children at Christmas, along with anything else you care to mention. Voting sometimes took place there at local and national elections – it was the hub of our village.

The W.I. began the decade where they had been for many years in a small hut beside the Old Pond. However, in 1949, a new much larger meeting place was erected in what we then knew as the playing field at the Veryan Green end of the water garden. They had quite a large membership in those days as there were few other attractions for the ladies of an evening.

There were Cubs in Veryan until their leader Mrs Croggan left the village. Mr Bunny ran a pack for a while just after the war and I recall going to a third pack about 1948, there was just one meeting. The pack I joined had meetings in the infant's class at the school when one boy brought his tea in an Oxo Tin. I recall buying that boy's three wheel bike for five shillings, only to give it back to his big sister who told mum they couldn't do without it.

After the war tourists began arriving. They travelled down by train and either hired a taxi or caught the bus to the village. Local residents were joined by servicemen who had married local girls and the odd land girl who had wed local farmers. The war had brought a great many evacuees to Veryan it had become better because of this. New faces arrived at both ends of the village, slow at first but it would quicken before too long.

There were three places of worship in Veryan then; the parish church along with two Methodist Chapels at Trewartha and Ebenezer. The shell of the latter still stands on the top of a hill going towards Calendra. Trewartha Chapel has been turned into a dwelling house; it has been done with care. The church and Trewartha had Sunday schools where strong in the early forties, during the war, but they dwindled later. My father was a steward at the Chapel and superintendent of the Sunday school, followed by Mr Pill of Camels. Mum played the organ there for many years; it was also played by Mrs Rundle who did this at the Sunday school. The war years were marked by the singing, almost every Sunday, of the hymn, *Father in Thy Mercy*.

It would have been just after the war when a Mr Grose who sometimes came to preach, started coming to host social evenings. He used to bring a box of doughnuts I recall. When refreshment time came round these were placed in the middle of the room. He did the same at Port Holland and I remember two or three of us boys going there with him once. The Christian faith, so much the cornerstone of my life, was being instilled in me during those dark days. Our vicar during the war was Mr Alston, who liked shooting, ferreting etc. He kept a Dalmatian along with gun dogs possibly. It was during the war years when he came in school wearing his surplus. On seeing him one little girl began to cry. When a teacher asked what was she crying for, her reply *"Tes the ol' pason, I daunt like the look ab um,"* he was with his mother and a housekeeper Miss Brown. Mr Alston often came into the school to see

Mr Bennett. His successor always arrived to take prayers at 9 a.m. on Thursdays. I cannot recall going to the church much during my time at school, about once a year. Different Ministers oversaw the Roseland Circuit of which the local chapels were part. Mr Eagle, Mr Simon, Mr Race and Pastor Owen, then finally Mr Le Poidevin who saw us into a new decade. Two Deaconesses were also in the circuit for a while. I seem to recall a Pastor Rickard marrying my uncle and aunt in 1943, think he lived at Tregongon. It rained cats and dogs all that day. Some of the pews were removed from the parish church in the early forties because of deathwatch beetle. I believe these were sold in the school playground.

What of national events – how were they celebrated in Veryan? V.E. Day I recall vaguely, mainly the five Union Flags sent to us by the mother of our evacuees. My granny made a square handle for them, covered these with old sheets, fastened the flags to these and we hung one from each window. I recall listening to Princess Elizabeth's wedding on the radio on November 20th 1947, which was my 11th birthday.

They sang, 'The Lords My Shepherd' to the tune Crimond.

Chapter Two

THE 1950S

The decade began with the deaths of some older inhabitants which meant houses having different occupiers or owners. The first to die was my grandmother who had lived in the cottage next down from the roundhouse. My grandparents had rented the house the summer of 1950, my uncle and aunt bought it and moved in. They also purchased the two small ones beside it. About eighteen months later a doctor's widow bought two from them and made them one. She named it Roseland Cottage, a name it has retained to this day. She then purchased three of the next block, where the second house was empty. The tenants in the first one were moved into it and theirs done up and let for holidays.

The one let by the doctor's widow however was lived in again by the end of the fifties when a Mrs Gilbert bought it. The bottom house also lost its owner, who with her late husband had at one time owned eight houses. Her death saw that become a third holiday home, having been purchased by a Dr. Walker. The lower cottage of block three became vacant with the passing of Mr Hearle and a new tenant, Mrs Frost arrived, her sharp tongue gave the fussy landlord a few shocks. The gentleman in the first house with a glass porch died, whereupon the place became the property of first, Mrs Pill of Camels who very soon sold it to my uncle who was a decorator, he named it Lamorna. The end house in the row was bought by a Dr Rutherford, another second home. Sunflower Cottage as it now is, also became a holiday home. This followed the death of Miss Rundle, the tenants of Sunflower having been moved into her place. The people who lived in the block of thatched houses, resided in one and let the other during the season. That's how second homes first started in Veryan Green.

Ten more council houses were built down in Veryan itself, adding to the two put up pre-war and the six built in the late forties. The Homeyard Homes, for fishermen's widows, were built in the mid fifties. This consisted of six homes for widows and one for the matron. The first occupants were as follows: Mrs Cox, Mrs Teague, Mrs Berry, Mrs Ellis, Mrs Gregory, along with Mrs Trudgeon and her young son.

The first matron was Mrs Jessop with her husband looking after the garden. Later in the fifties Miss Rollin took over as matron and my uncle, Mr Alf Lagor, spent three days a week in the garden. Much more building would take place in the future.

The parish saw a building which brought another business when Mr J.J. Harris put up a garage at Bessie Beneath and moved there in 1956. Another new business began late in the decade when at Mr Trist's death his estate was split up, with Parc Be-han being sold to Mr Askew from Sussex. He named the place Veryan Green Hotel and a large board was erected to advertise the fact. Mr Peter Royds, a very tall gentleman, became its manager. A business was lost when Miss Rundle passed away, but a new grocer arrived when the Lea family went. Her name was Mrs Mack, a real tough cookie, she had run a pub in the East End of London and named the house Welsley Cottage after it. Her animals consisted of a large ginger cat, an even bigger dog and a great many budgerigars. Her lodger (Bill) was sent one day to collect the debts, ringing in his ears were her warning words 'Mind you don't come back without them,' her bark though was worse than her bite and she was kind to me on many occasions. It was during her time here the old stone shed with carpenter's shop above was made into a garage for two cars. She had purchased it from Miss Rundle's relative. Roseland Stores changed hands twice during the fifties and a newcomer, Miss Langan, took over what is now known as Grannie's Attic, where she displayed and sold knitwear.

Three businessmen passed away in 1959; Mr Elliott the butcher, Mr Reynolds, who had a small farm and went each Thursday with his horse and wagon to Portloe selling vegetables. His death was to prove significant for the future of house building in Veryan. The third death that year was Mr Augustus Davis who had been a builder for many years in the village. He was ninety when he died and was I'm sure still working in the forties.

Farming was still the main source of employment for men but the disease myxomatosis put paid to the trapping of rabbits for a living. This meant the end of Tonkin's lorry arriving in the village each day to pick them up. The end of so many rabbits was a blessing for farmers and growers alike. It was also a blessing for me as I'd started growing vegetables for a living after leaving school. The farmers had help too the hay and corn harvests along with the milking along being partly taken over

Fordson Tractor.

1940s

Traditional Cornish Range.

I

Veryan's War Memorial.

1940s

Veryan school's canteen.

II

Time for crowst during harvesting at Treburthas.

1950s

Cattle at Treburthas.

Homeyard Homes.

1950s

The Jet garage.

The old butchers shop.

1960s

A 1960s bungalow, which was the first one built in Veryan Green.

Portscatho doctor surgery.

1960s

A classic of the 1960s, a Morris Minor 1300, the same as the nurse drove.

Roseland Gardens.

1970s

Changes to the Triangle at Veryan Green.

VII

Caravan park.

1970s

Art gallery.

by machines that milked the cows, baled the hay and combined the corn. A new crop, Silage, came on the scene; it would become very popular as it was less dependent on dry weather to harvest than hay. Artificial Insemination for cows had come in the previous decade, which saved my dad walking in season cows to a farm at Tippets. Some farmers grew sugar beet, which were loaded into lorries with special forks and taken to the station. Many hedges were grubbed out and gateways widened to accommodate the machinery. I can think of cases where three fields were made into one. Some boys still had their first job on a farm while others I'd been at school with went to learn to be either masons or carpenters at Portscatho with Nickolls and Nickolls, another went all the way to St Mawes with a man named Madron. They all travelled by bicycle until they had saved enough to buy a motor-cycle. The lad who learnt plumbing walked several miles to pick up two bicycles which he made into one so he could get to his job. Apprentices were paid very low wages which gradually improved, as they got older. On the farm my dad worked for £1 a day in 1955.

When mains water arrived in 1953 many men found casual employment. They did have a machine with which to cut the road and a tamper with which to bang down the rubble returned when pipes had been laid. In between there was much hard graft with pick and shovel. There was more hard work when a few houses were sold to people who wanted a bathroom for which septic tanks were built after more digging. There was one in the allotment I seem to remember.

Most of the girls were moving away from the traditional household chores and going in for hairdressing, typing etc. A workers bus was started in which they travelled to Truro each day. At eighteen, or at the completion of an apprenticeship, young men had to do two years National Service unless they worked on a farm. Two of the boys with whom I was at school joined the Royal Marines for a longer period. Another who had come here as an evacuee chose the Royal Air Force, while one or two left Veryan to join the police and others found employment further afield. The lure of work further away was beginning to have some effect,

17

partly as more people now had transport, be it in some cases only a motor-cycle.

At Veryan School, Mr Bennett was still in charge but after twenty years this would be his final decade. It was during the fifties the Inter School Sports began. There were more new teachers; Miss Lane, Mrs Williams, Mrs Greet again for a short spell, Mr Taylor remained and a new infant teacher Mrs Unsworth arrived in 1952. Meals were now eaten in the Legion Hall, with a new lady cooking them after Mrs Moses left Veryan. The new cook was Mrs Stoneman, who as Miss Dowrick, had of course helped Mrs Moses. She was in fact married while helping her. I have rarely ate after a better cook than Mrs Moses. Her jam paste and heavy cake could often be had during afternoon break if there was any left.

Very early in that decade, when I was nearly 14 years old, some new desks arrived. A yellow table replaced Mr Bennett's old box desk, and I was among the few lucky pupils who got a new one. In 1951, the year I left, a trip was organised to Paignton Zoo. Some time before that a Mrs Champion came to teach the girls sewing, while older boys went to Truro for carpentry classes. At the close of that decade Mr Bennett finally retired and left the village for retirement at Sticker. Having taught both parents and their children in some cases he knew the history of many pupils. There had been many interests other than the school involving him in many organisations. The church, autumn show, British Legion and Parish Council. Those of us who were his pupils still refer to him as Sir, and recall his little sayings with pleasure. He led by example and I cannot recall ever seeing him without a collar and tie. He addressed the other teachers as Mr, Mrs or Miss as he wanted us to do. It's said he wasn't a good teacher, that's not my opinion, but I remember him most of all for the good influence he had on me. Despite him telling us many times, we were duffers, few of us left not able to read and write, and we have gone on to be honest citizens. I can recall going to vote at the school for the first time in 1959. When I emerged having cast my vote he was standing having a chat with someone. He gave me a look and said, 'I hope you voted for the right man Frank.' There was at that election a lady standing as well. I've often smiled to myself about this as I voted for the lady.

18

The Legion hall underwent changes with electricity being installed. This meant better lighting and an electric boiler with which to heat the water. This replaced the enormous kettles which used to be boiled on the open fires. The weights and measures officers came each July; when local farmers brought their scales to be tested and I took my spring balance. I recall going to a wedding reception there along with some of the plays put on by the first Veryan Players. Their first, I think in 1956, caused a stir when Mr Lee Dodds our new vicar took part and had some swearing among his lines. The first play I went to see was called 'Easy Money,' the one that caused offence, 'Castles In The Air.' I believe those taking part used a caravan parked outside as a dressing room and climbed in through the window.

Mr Dodds had replaced Mr Mapplebeck as vicar. The mid fifties saw the opening of a new piece of land to be used for burials. This at the back of Homeyard Homes was first used in 1955, I think. New pews were installed down the centre of the church, to replace those removed in the forties. The Sunday School at Trewartha closed, as did Ebenezer Chapel, which Miss Rundle had striven so hard to keep going. Mr Winter was the Methodist minister for one year when Mr La Poivdevin went. Then Mr Race returned for a second spell. A Circuit Harvest Festival was started as were Friday night fellowship meetings in 1954. Mr Race left in 1958 to be followed by Mr Bailey. He didn't have a car but rode a scooter instead causing one old lady to call him, 'Old Tin Hat.'

The W.I. was still strong, as was the Cricket Club now playing in a field near Trewartha Chapel.

Veryan could have fielded three teams at the time but soon moved to Mr Elliott's field just up the main road from the turning leading to Trewartha from Veryan Green. The first team consisted mainly of men from the Tregunna, Kendall and Johns families, with a few exceptions. There had been a football team in the late forties but it didn't last long. There had also been badminton played in the Legion hall in that decade.

Early in the decade a pavement was laid beside the cottages, down through Veryan Green, with the road having been made higher already, this meant most of them now had steps down from the gate. The pillarbox was also moved across the road where it still remains. The fence between the field and allotment was trimmed but the number of men working there was falling. This wasn't helped when the Tregunna family left for a council house in Veryan. Mr Tregunna, who had lost a leg in the Great War, planted three plots with the sale of produce part of his livelihood. I often think with hindsight how brave he was, an example to many folk now. Artificial legs in those days weren't like they are now, but he earned a living. His taxi which stood outside his door by the telephone pole and Mr Channon's van were the only ones parked by the roadside. An increase in cars was to bring a gradual increase in the numbers seen parked in this way. More cars all over the country meant more tourists, of which my mum took in a few for B&B. We got some interesting characters, including three ladies who slept in one bed. Two married couples who would have slept in the same room had mum allowed such a thing. A couple who brought a boat on a trailer which dad assured would break down, and it did. A family named Rugg with a girl and boy, Andria and Neal. The latter had every complaint in the world, when he didn't want to go home. Then there were the Snow's who dad had to put off when mums ulcer broke. The lady, who had run away from her husband, had a private detective trailing her. And a family called Mulliner with a girl named Christine, the husband called Eric I think, played cricket for a visitor's team against Veryan. I also took them to the Nare Head to fly a kite. The best entertainment, though frustrating for mum, came in 1959.

An ex-barrister who had left the village recently came and asked could he have bed and breakfast for a time. Mum agreed, not realising his knowledge of the law would be used to embarrass her. While he stayed she could only take couples. If more came than could be accommodated he would say, 'Can't take them,' he also told mum she couldn't turn him out while that board was advertising B&B. Mother had booked a party of four in August – they needed two bedrooms. So a couple slept in rooms either side of mine, mum and dad on a put-you-up in the kitchen, and the other gentleman in the sitting room. This wouldn't have been so bad had he not put the radio on at six each morning. When sleeping upstairs he would throw the water used to wash out of the window. He ended up having dinner with us as well telling mum the lady who had been feeding him bought her meat by the yard. The doorway of her house was low and he often swore about knocking his head. But, back to the party of four and the biggest laugh of all. Mum was going to give them roast chicken with blackberry and apple pie to follow. He offered to pick the blackberries if he could have some of the meal. When evening came he sat full of expectation as mum took in the chicken etc. His mood soon changed when told they had eaten the lot. When they cleared the pie as well he called them a variety of names including, 'Guts.'

The Tregunna family moved to Veryan council estate which meant no taxi at Veryan Green, though Mr Rawling and his son had two taxis. The buses were still packed each time they went to Truro or St Austell and there were still queues at the cinema of a Saturday evening. The bus left at 10.15 pm and we sometimes missed the end of a film in our desire to buy fish and chips at Lang's shop in Truro. Sometimes running with them in order to catch the bus. Trips were run by the bus owners for the many tourists who had no car; St Mawes twice weekly in order to catch the ferry to Falmouth. Lands End and the Lizard were visited weekly and there were mystery trips of an evening. One old chap I knew called them *'misery trips.'* These trips became less as more tourists came in their own cars. In 1955 Mr Tregunna sold his bus to Mr Morse and went to work in the Council yard as a mechanic. He had purchased it several years before from his cousin who now had a taxi. Mr Truscott at Ruan Highlanes also had a blue and grey bus with which he transported children to school in Truro. I believe he sold the business during that decade to a Mr Fox.

I recall vividly the death of our late King George VI on February 6th 1952. Queen Elizabeth's Coronation the following year remains even more clearly in the memory.

It was the custom in Veryan to have a meat tea. To that end, a Hereford bullock was killed in the killing house of yesteryear, on Mr Melville Rundles land. During the week before this took place his workman and I cleared the house of manure whitened the walls and scrubbed the floor. On the evening of May 29th the bullock was killed by Mr Alf Julyan, having been caught and hauled into the house. Two or three of us boys carried the water and were told by Mr Julyan, 'Come Tuesday you shall have all the *'mate'* you can ate.'

On Tuesday morning, 2nd June 1953, came news that Edmond Hillary and Sherpa Tensing had conquered Everest. Later that morning I listened with bated breathe to the coronation ceremony, then in the early afternoon went first to a service at the church, followed by the tea, and sports. The day ended with a bonfire in the field by Jubilee Corner, near Trethenal Gate. It was very cold, the bonfire was lit by Mr Augustus Davis.

Chapter Three

THE 1960s

Early in the decade the land that had been farmed by the late Mr Reynolds was sold. Later in the sixties it was sold again, this time for building. The first of 32 bungalows were already lived in when the decade ended. Bay House was sold and took the name Elerkey House Hotel, after the Elerkey estate, which owned much of Veryan in years gone by.

Mr Hearle who had lived in it as a farmhouse retired from farming and built a bungalow on his own land at the top end of the council estate. He sold the remainder of the four acre field to the council, hence that end being called Four Acres Road. Six old people's flats were built straight away. Two dwellings were also put up where Mr Reynolds' farmyard had been, just round the corner from Hillside. Two bungalows were built behind the Roseland Stores and one behind the school. Mr Buddle built a house for himself looking down onto the coal yard.

For much of that decade Elerkey House Hotel was owned by Mr and Mrs Donald Langford. Mr and Mrs Charles Cracknell moved with their family into The New Inn. Mr Fred Reynolds took over the piece of land vacated by Mr Bennett just up from the Roseland Stores. At the end of the sixties Mr Luke retired and Mr Buddle's brother took over his business. Mr Rawling senior passed away about the time his son began selling petrol.

At Veryan Green there were also plans afoot to build bungalows. The first, St Creda, was occupied late 1960. A damp bit of land that had been occupied by Mr Tregunna's poultry was sold by the new owner of what's now called The Shambles. The early sixties saw three bungalows erected there. A garage was built by Mr Conway on what had been an orchard just above The Shambles. Mr Conway who lived in the block of thatched cottages soon passed away, whereupon his cottages were sold and named Mabetwin. Later in the decade a bungalow was put up beside it. Another was put up in the field opposite, along with an agricultural one down the short lane beyond. Mr Channon built one for himself, now called 'Sun Cloud,' with his new wife he first lived there in March 1964. Sunflower was sold and permanent residents moved in during January 1966. Before it was sold along with what's now called Jim Jons, their back gardens were sold for building, and a bungalow named The Shealing went up. Dr

Walker sold Pentilie to Lady Williams in 1966 who later bought a round house in Veryan. The house where our headmaster had lived was sold to a family named Neal, the son was M.P. for North Cornwall. The Hampshire family took over the Post Office where they lived at Trevurbin House having moved here from Yorkshire. Mr Hampshire was taken ill and in 1969, the Post Office moved to the Roseland Stores.

The above mentioned Roseland stores had three owners during that decade, or was it four? Mr Levers, Mr Bankier, Mrs Lewis and Mr Harvey George. The Post Office moved there in 1969 near Christmas, with Mrs Lewis selling up soon after. Mr Bankier started selling Spar products and Mrs Lewis, Sunday papers. Mr Gerry Buddle took over Mr Luke's coal business while living in a mobile home below the school yard. Mrs Mack went about 1969, and the place had a spell empty. Ollerearnshaw & Symons started a building business also in 1969. The Truscott brothers set up a butchers business in 1960. They built a new shop near Pendower Road and I opened my first greengrocers shop at Veryan Green. Ivor Buddle set up as a builder and David Harris set up in business as a plumber. Mrs Lewis took over Grannies Attic for a while about 1968.

We had a new police house built on the corner between Pendower Road and Four Acres Road; the first officer to live in it was Mr Ollerearnshaw. He was followed later in the sixties by Mr Gilbert.

Nurse Surley retired soon after a car replaced her bicycle, and Nurse Scott arrived. A very small lady, who drove a Morris car.

Our medical service underwent great changes when a new surgery was built at Portscatho late in the decade. At which point our once weekly surgery in Veryan came to an end, it had been held on Thursday afternoons at three different abodes: Trenison Bungalow, Treviskey and Camels but not in that order. I can also recall going with a friend to see Dr Scott at his home near Rosevine. About the same time the health service took over a council house in Veryan in which the new St Mawes nurse was to reside. Her name was Edwards and she replaced Nurse Wheeler who had helped the St Mawes doctor for many years in 1976. We'd had a trainee doctor since the spring of 1964, the first being Dr Laing.

Civil defence came to Veryan with a hut being erected and an underground bunker near the Nare Head. Several local young men joined and met in the hut. I can recall some of them wearing coats with the word 'Rescue' on the shoulder,

At the school Mr Gotch followed Mr Bennett as head. Mr Taylor went to the comprehensive at Tregony for a while before he in turn became

24

head at Veryan. The big school at Tregony made a difference to our village school as every child went there automatically at 11 years of age.

The National Trust became the owners of Gwendra Farm and rented the beach very early in the sixties. They let the land and converted the house into two flats. A car park was made between Tirva and the next dwelling with a man engaged to take the money. The mid sixties found them running Parc – Behan as well. The house was turned into four flats with a couple named Frampton arriving as caretakers early in 1967. Two of the flats were let on a permanent basis – a third weekly, with the Framptons right at the top. The little cottage round the back was also let weekly. Mr Frampton looked after the beach while his wife did the odd day at the car park. They also did the change overs at their own place and at Gwendra. There was anger among some of the locals who had never paid to park their cars before but charges didn't last long and an honesty box replaced the attendant in due course. This parking area was much needed as before it arrived people parked all over the place. One of the fruit wholesalers who came to me also went to the Nare Hotel. On one occasion he couldn't get near the hotel for cars. Knowing his produce was needed, he went down to the beach, found the owners and asked them to shift the offending cars.

Late in that decade mains sewerage arrived, Veryan was at long last getting modern. Their machines made an awful mess of the lane outside Mrs Mack's, and a rather cross shop keeper gave me a letter to post off to the firm Bazeleys. They responded by sending loads of small stones, which were never comfortable to walk on. That must have been not long before she went from the village.

Very late in the decade, a snooker table was given by a recent arrival to the Legion Hall. Those outside the Legion, who wished to use it, could join as associate members. Johnny Baron came from Mevagissey to open the table. The Veryan Players folded about 1966, in fact I recall going to their last effort in the spring of that year. Joan Blamey played the part of a character named Laura. With her mother, she had just returned from visiting her sister and first child, who had joined her husband who was in the Black Watch regiment there.

The Roseland Methodists saw changes when Mr Bailey left and Dr Beckerlegg arrived. It was decided a summer fete was needed to raise some much needed cash. Our minister wanted somebody famous to open it. After some debate it was decide, to seek one of the stars from the radio programme *The Archers*. Bob Arnold, who played the part of Tom Forrest, actually came and did the honours. 1968 saw another change of minister when Mr Hayes arrived. He would be the last minister to live at the Manse at St Mawes. The

25

year after he arrived boys from Cliff College visited our circuit and made their headquarters at Trewartha Sunday School. A wonderful coloured gentleman named Esaw came with them. He stayed with the Elliotts at Trethenal Farm. I remember how pleased I was at the way those young men treated him. They called him Sunshine, which his lovely smile reminded me of. The fete that year was opened by Mrs C Warne, a farmer's wife from Tregony. Two Deaconesses, Sister Ivy and Sister Jennifer also came during that decade. New ideas were needed to raise money, one of which was a circuit concert. My best memory of this was the brilliant piano playing of Mrs Hayes, the minister's wife. It was also Mrs Hayes who started the circuit choir. Male voice choirs gave concert, during June for some years at Trewatha Chapel. I can recall Treverva, Holman Climax and the Nankersy coming.

The cricket club made a marvellous start to the decade, when in 1961 they won the senior east and took part in the final at Camborne. I remember going with a relative when Veryan took the field in blazing sunshine. They had a hard time there as Cyril Calaway knocked up a century in a large total by Camborne. Tea was taken before the Veryan innings began but fog enveloped the ground and play was called off. I think the game was replayed and Veryan lost. In 1965 we were again doing well and I recall in July going with them to play at Wadebridge, having fish & chips, and going into a pub on the way home. I went with Mr Fred Lagor and Mr Jim Johns in his grandson Clifford's car. They all had alcohol, while I, the odd man out, had bitter lemon. On August 21st Veryan played St Minver at home and sitting beside Mr Hubert Whitford, on a seat just inside the gate. England were playing the final Test against South Africa, for whom Colin Bland made a century. It was to be their last tour here for many years. And everyone remembers England's win in the World Cup of 1966. Most people now had television and could watch such things as they happened.

Television also allowed us to watch a big national event – the funeral of Sir Winston Churchill, the great war leader to whom everyone owed so much. Heads of state came from many countries in honour of the great man, who, during the war years had kept the nation going with speeches of determination and defiance. Some of his words will live forever in the history of this country. *'Never in the field of human conflict have so many owed so much to so few'* and the words which when war had ended shifted the praise on to ordinary folk, when he said, *'This is your victory.'* Without him there would have been no victory, for it was he who drove us on. The state funeral awarded so rarely to a commoner, was a fitting tribute to one of the greatest Englishmen. Certainly the greatest of my lifetime.

Chapter Four

THE 1970S

The decade opened with much building work going on. Eight more council houses and four old people's flats were under construction at Four Acres Road. The bungalows at Roseland Gardens were completed. Late in the seventies work began on another almost opposite named Elerkey Close Estate. A bungalow was being built by Mr Buddle next to St Creda at Veryan Green while fifty yards away Wayside was having an extension added for my family to move into. The bungalow was first lived in during December 1970, we arrived at Wayside the following march and the council tenants arrived in August the same year. I will attempt to name them. Miss Kendall, Mr and Mrs Alf Lagor, Mr and Mrs Fred Scoffield and Mr and Mrs Dowrick in old folks' flats. Houses looking down on garages. Mr and Mrs Reg Kendall, Mrs Johns, her son and Miss Johns, Mrs Reynolds and son, Mrs Fred Lagor and his two sisters. Third block looking at backs of those in Pendower Road, the Ball family, the Harris family, the Symons family and the Couch family. Soon after this a bungalow was started round the corner from Hillside for another Johns family, followed by one next to the butchers shop for the newly weds Paul and Pauline Truscott. Two bungalows were also put up in what we called No-Mans Land.

Two years later at Veryan Green Mr Millington built one the other side of St Creda and Miss Langan put one up on the other side of the road. On top of all that Mr W Channon built his house behind Sea Cloud.

The house we had left at the top of the Green was bought by the Spital's and the out buildings became an art gallery. Where Mrs Mack had been became in turn grocers, restaurant and hair dressing salon before finally closing as a business in 1978. Ivor Buddle took over the coal business from his brother and the Roseland Stores changed hands at least twice. Mr Harvey George sold to the Lockyer's who brought a Mrs Billingsley with them she went to live in Tregony. The Lockyers in turn sold to the Prichards. God knows who had Grannies Attic by now. On moving to Four Acres Mrs Reynolds gave up her vegetable customers to whom she had taken goods by hand since the horse died.

There were changes for most people in business with decimalisation and V.A.T. both coming our way. The first on February 15th 1971 was easy though I managed to give a customer the wrong change on the first day. V.A.T. a bit later was not so easy but as with most things we got accustomed to filling out the form in time.

The Conservative government elected in 1970 set up a ministry of the environment. They launched a scheme to tidy up Britain for which grants were available. Veryan obtained one with which the triangle of grass at Veryan Green was lowered, the corner rounded at Wayside End, and grass seeds sown. The patch of land opposite the Legion Hall was drained, as was the land where children's swings etc are. Although those pieces were drained they never go brown no matter how dry the weather.

My father went to work part time at Homeyard Homes in the summer of 1971. He finished working part-time on farms in October 1972 and took on the job of keeping the churchyard tidy. He also worked a couple of days a week for others, his pay ten shillings (50p) an hour. A certain gentleman named Dingle paid more when dad assisted him. During the baking hot summer of 1976 he used to begin work at 6 a.m. and finish at ten.

A little more on the price of goods. When my shop was built, concrete blocks were one shilling (five pence) each and cement 13 shillings or 65 pence per hundredweight.

Mr Taylor retired as head at the school to be replaced by the Rev. Dorrington in 1971. As his title suggests he was also able to conduct services in the church. Another new teacher, Mrs Hutchins came, Mrs Harold Tregunna was cook for a time, she lived in the village, the first to do so since Mr Bennett. Mrs Hutchins was also a teacher. There was a short period before the new head arrived, during which Mrs Unsworth and her sister took charge.

The W.I. didn't have so many members, and a new organization for older people called The Good Companions was started by Mr and Mrs Parsons, who had recently come here to live. This was something completely new in Veryan, though some villages had such organizations for some time. It seemed a good idea and would help the many retired people who had come here to pass time.

There were girl guides in Veryan which was also a good thing. Cubs and scouts had their headquarters at Trewartha Chapel. The W.I. market was started for one hour each Friday.

Miss Margery Johns retired as our post lady after thirty years service. Having cycled from Portloe six days a week in all weathers. There were scores of tourists and a new caravan park was opened at Tretheake. It was a modern outfit with toilet block, shop, fishing lake etc. But seemed to make little difference to the two other sites in farmer's fields. These were overlooking Carne beach and Port Holland. The boiling hot summer of 1976 saw scores of caravans, tents etc. One or two people began to fuss which was the beginning of the end for these sites in farmer's fields. Though the one I often visited at Carne was always tidy.

I went to the new surgery for the first time in October 1971 with a bad tooth. There was a secretary behind a cubby hole and a waiting room, which was pleasant and warm. The doctor referred me to a dentist, just up the road. That has changed a bit too, but then I hadn't been since I was at school. A tooth was extracted and I felt nothing. Blimey, I thought some things have certainly changed for the better. Nurse Scott retired and a Nurse Dunning arrived. She lived with her mother in the house vacated by Nurse Edwards. But not for long, as Nurse Wood took her place in the area and lived there for a few months before moving to Gerrans.

There was a Dr Mcluer here for sometime. I believe he came from Worcestershire. I also recall a trainee named Dr Clark, who I think had been in the Royal Navy.

Trewartha Chapel was now stronger than for some years! There was an increase in the congregation, with some of them coming from Rosevine. Flush toilets and other improvements were carried out in a scheme involving Manpower Services.

In the early months of 1979 Veryan lost several of its parishioners. Some twelve I think passed away in the first two months. One could only reach the doctor's surgery at Portscatho in a four-wheel drive vehicle. I believe that was the year our doctor and nurse had to seek help in their efforts to see many patients. On top of which our milkman, who lived at Portloe, couldn't get out of that village for six days. When he did manage to get here it was with the help of a farmer and his tractor. It had started to snow on New Years Eve. Very late that year

Mr Charles Cracknell retired from the New Inn. Many years in the Royal Navy made him a wonderful choice to lay the wreath on Remembrance Sunday.

Of course the main national event was the Queen's Silver Jubilee celebrations in early June 1977. Meetings were held here for months prior to the event. As I recall, the main difference from previous big occasions, was that salad was to be had with the customary meat tea. The animal had to be slaughtered properly this time at a slaughterhouse and I believe the meat was cooked at the Lugger Hotel, Portloe. The usual church service was held in the afternoon followed by sports. A new cross-country race was introduced, which took the runners up through the wood on Mr Rundle's land. The sports were held in his field below the wood. Mugs were presented to the children by Mr Bennett who had been headmaster at Veryan School such a long time. Miss Jenkin made a speech in which she thanked Mr Rundle for letting his land be used, and spoke of always having a meat tea in Veryan. As on all such occasions I felt proud to be British. I should add at this point how Miss Jenkin had arrived in the parish during the early thirties and took an active part in its affairs.

The Jubilee celebrations were so successful many people wanted something similar the next year. And so it was that the Veryan Gala Week arrived. It became very popular with folk coming from many miles to see the Carnival on the closing Saturday. I recall among other things a Donkey Derby and a Circus.

Chapter Five
THE 1980S

The decade was only five months old when the first bungalow at Elerkey Close was completed. Getting out the foundations had taken some time due to an old mine working being discovered. At the turn of the decades another Mr Johns built a home nearby. Melinsey Farm as we had known it would be no more, for the last people who farmed it sold two of the best fields. One to another farmer, the second to the parish, it would be used as a sports ground and social club, of which I will speak more later. A Doctor Clynick bought the house along with the Water Mill and some land. Mr Morley Johns had a bungalow built between his brother and Elerkey Close. At Veryan Green the property now known as Tamarand Thatch was split into two when Mr and Mrs Seals bought the place in 1983. The part that had always been a business was sold separately to a Mr Naylor who later sold to Mr Cope. About 1986 he submitted plans to turn it into a dwelling, which he did giving it the name Tamerand Date. Mrs Nickolls who had lived in the row opposite my shop all her life started falling about and had to go into a home in 1985. After some renovation her house along with next door which she used as a store, both became holiday homes. This meant that five of the seven cottages in that row were no longer lived in on a permanent basis.

The Roseland Stores had yet more owners: the Harringtons followed by the Armstrongs and Platts. Mr Truscott retired from the butchers shop and was followed by his nephew David and his wife. David's father who went round with a van, having finished five years earlier. Stuart Rawling also retired handing over to his son Michael. He was the third generation of that family to run a business there. Morse's buses stopped going to Truro after the death of Mr Morse senior. He had been driving a bus for sixty years but it was no longer economic to do so. Veryan people now went on Lidgey's bus from Tregony. David Harris, the plumber, left Veryan after an illness. Mothers Pride stopped delivering bread and the camp sites at Carne and Tregenna closed. Only the one at Tretheake remained that was sold mid decade to two ladies.

The biggest change in our medical care came in the autumn of 1981. For the first time since the first war we didn't have a doctor called Scott. Dr Frank who arrived during that war had been followed by his son Dr Keith. So when he retired it was for many of us the end of an era. My generation had never had a doctor by any other name. My late mother always recalled how he had carried her from his surgery to Mr Rawlings, car at the time her ulcer burst. She had been a mere girl when his father first arrived. Dr Price who arrived in Veryan five years earlier took over his patients, myself included. Mr Louttit, the dentist at Gerrans, also retired, I'm including him because of the great kindness he showed me at a time when dentists made me nervous. That kindness included two visits to my home, one unpaid, which I will never forget. My dad did some work for him during the seventies and was treated well. I would also like to mention before leaving medical care the kindness shown by all at the surgery at the time when both my parents were seriously ill in 1989.

At the school numbers were getting low and there was anxiety every year over the possible loss of a teacher. Mr Dorrington left in 1984 to be replaced by the first woman head Mrs Carlhausen. She in turn was succeeded by Miss Trythall in 1988. After twenty eight years loyal service Mrs Unsworth retired. Like Mr Bennett, Mr Taylor and Miss Pascoe before her, he taught a great many children. There were by now helpers at the school, working on a one to one basis with children with special needs being educated in mainstream schools. Children who had problems of any kind getting more assistance was one of the things which most pleased me. They didn't get it in my days there, and I was glad this had been put right. The children now went swimming each week and a new toilet block was opened. More young people were going on to further education, sixth form college and even university.

The vicarage, the vicarage lodge and a barn on Gleeb land were sold in three lots and a bungalow built for the new vicar. This was situated at the bottom of the old vicarage drive. Our new vicar, Mr Geach, arrived in 1984 and his induction took place on July 2nd. Cannon Geach, as he later became, was a tireless worker who rode his bicycle round Veryan parish.

The New Vicarage.

1980s

Elerkey Close.

Clubhouse.

1980s

Tennis Courts.

Barn conversion at Polcuta.

1990s

Melinsey Mill.

The Veryan School reunion cake 1999.

1990s

Former teacher, Mrs Unsworth, cutting the reunion cake with the author.

Changes to Veryan School.

2000s

Rundels Walk.

2000s

Wind turbine.

Veryan Church, and grave-yard – the site of the longest grave in the world. The grave holds twelve German sailors.

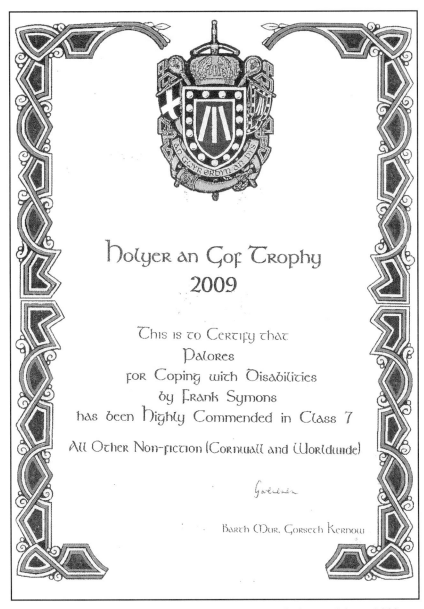

Palores Publications and the author's Holyer an Gof award from 2009.

He knew everyone and treated them all the same. Later in his life I was sad when told he had sight problems. A fine man with high principles he will long be remembered in Veryan. The old vicarage was renamed Trist House after the family who had done so much for the village. The lodge was renovated and the barn turned into a dwelling.

My mother played the organ at Trewartha Chapel for the last time in 1982 when she was taken there by car and knew the hymns before hand. She was presented with a tune book for long service which I still have. Miss Dowrick (Aunty Maud) had done the same thing at Veryan Church. To my shame I hadn't attended Chapel for many years, upset partly by the emphasis being more and more on money.

The Roseland Circuit in general was not in good shape, some chapels having closed.

The Legion Hall venue for so many events over many years would soon have competition. The new sports and social club was taking shape. A small group of volunteers gave freely of their time, clearing stones etc before building could even begin. But, building was only part of the work, as the bowling green also had to be prepared. Outdoor bowls began first, to be quickly followed by indoor. The cricket club at long last had a really good ground to play on but sadly there were few players. A tennis club was formed and our village had facilities many towns would be proud of. The clubhouse itself was the venue for many functions and pushed the Legion Hall into the background somewhat. The Royal British Legion branch here was not strong now and many of its members were getting old. Some of them played snooker of a Monday evening and there were a few associate members. I became one of these in 1986 and played twice a week.

Work trends were changing with less men on the land and others made redundant setting up as gardeners. This meant a lot more self-employed workers. Two newcomers went all the way to London to jobs, coming home at weekends. With all the new dwellings there were a great many fresh faces in the village, those of working age travelled quite a distance each day. Quite a few were professional people teachers, nurses and even a dentist. A lot more people now had part time jobs. The china clay industry gave men early retirement, with a lump sum and small pension. Many more wives were working, some full-time.

The big national event in 1981 was the wedding of Prince Charles and Lady Diana Spencer.

Chapter Six

THE 1990S

The main additions to the number of dwellings that decade were the 33 starter homes built on land left over from the piece purchased for Four Acres Road bought by the council in the early sixties. The work began early in 1993 when surplus soil was taken away in lorries. A friend of mine applied for one and showed me what the documents entailed: seventy-five per cent could be purchased with a mortgage, with the remainder paid as rent. The first person moved in on October 24th the same year. Though opposed by some, the estate did the village a service by bringing in young families, which in turn helped the school. Other building included barn conversions at Calendra Polcuta. The first was lived in at Polcuta in 1993 when Mr and Mrs Boxall moved in. About the same time a family named Cameron came to Calendra and lived in a caravan until the barn had been converted. The three conversions were to be known as Calendra Court, while Parc Vean Court was an appropriate name for those at Parc Vean.

The garage beside my shop was turned into a flat late in 1994 when I sold Wayside to the Hancock family. The old watermill at Melinsey was also being renovated. The vicarage lodge and old barn nearby were now lived in. The Salmon family moved into the old vicarage now known as Trist House in 1994. They hired men to clean up the large gardens which were to be opened on certain days to the public. The family also rented Grannies Attic for five years. Dr and Mrs Craige had renovated the old barn and moved in some time before. Tretheake Caravan Park was purchased by a camping and caravan club when one of the ladies running it died suddenly.

Things were not easy for people running a business with the number of vans coming round selling goods having been reduced to a trickle. I closed my greengrocers shop, as did Mr Truscott. So there was now only the one shop selling food, this compared to five in the sixties. The garage which had been run by the Rawling family for decades also closed. The other run by the Morse family was pulled down and a bungalow put in its place. The haulage business had gone, and the shed which had been its base, was getting rusty. These businesses were replaced to a certain degree by new ones; The Richards' brothers, April & Ben Bennett and Simon Burley. Mark Hawkins was another. But perhaps the most significant was the opening of Melinsey Mill by the Hancock family. Rickard, the husband, had restored the place and had it working as when corn was ground there. The opening took place in 1996 the family having purchased my house two years before. With a flair for making things, Rickard went on a basket making course and soon was making all kinds of things from willow. A workshop was erected near his dwelling house where he also made furniture. There were now so many rules and regulations, form filling and red tape. The final straw for many came early in the decade. Now food regulations meant visits from an inspector from the Environmental Heath Office. On his first visit he told me to make improvements which cost £155 while the second time I was asked how old the eggs were. When told I got them from a lady each Wednesday and didn't know their age his reply was, 'Well the lady should know how old they are.' He was pleasant enough but I thought the remark silly. Hygiene courses were available at £20 each, and many business people rushed to attend. I didn't bother and the officer told me years later they still weren't legally binding. I finally gave up my greengrocery business on November 30th 1996. A few weeks later Mr Truscott stopped selling meat. The Roseland Stores had no less than four owners during the nineties. The Platt family, David and Angela, Arthur and Sue, then finally Richard & Gillian. The Gravers moved into Elerkey House Hotel and promptly change it to Elerkey Guesthouse which I thought more appropriate. Mike & Alison Rawling sold the garage site for building, and moved to Trevurbyn House where Alison had lived as a girl in the sixties.

Men on farms were almost non-existent and there were very few going to work in the clay industry. The number of farms had also dwindled to about a quarter of what they were in the forties. Smaller ones were being taken over to make big ones larger on a regular basis. Milking herds had virtually vanished with the few who did milk keeping hundreds of cows. Almost every job was now done by a machine, with a farmer able to run a great many acres on his own.

Coal fires in many homes had also disappeared; being replaced by oil, electricity or central heating. This meant running a home was easier too, as did all the other equipment now available. With the cost of oil, water and electricity all rising along with the mortgages many people now found it necessary for more and more wives to work. With the addition of foreign holidays and meals out life was getting expensive for those who indulged in such things. I guess this was yet another sign of how much better off people in general were. For instance when I was young people struggled to buy even a bicycle and cars were only for the well off. I look around me now and see two and sometimes three cars to a house. The way folk dress gives another clue whereas in my youth most people only had two outfits now they have twenty. Few children wear handed down clothes and I don't suppose there are boys with only one pair of boots to their name. The fact people are better off pleases me and I'm only writing this to make my point.

The general lack of respect doesn't please many of my generation though. I hear people refer to teachers by their first name, or we didn't know their first names when I was at school. The vicar too is Dick, Tom or Harry, and even the doctor. When I hear a three year old call an old lady of ninety by her first name it makes me furious. However, I don't blame the child, but the adults who should know better than to do it in front of children. In all the time I was at Veryan School not once did I hear Mr Bennett do this. And why didn't he do so? Because he didn't want us copying him. However, I recall getting equally cross in days gone by when people referred to folk they felt beneath them by surnames only. It used to make me hopping mad and I would think, 'Who the devil do they think they are? In my Christian world people are all the same and I have no place in my life for racists or folk who look down on others. We can't all be rich nor can everyone be academic, but rich or poor, black, brown or white we all have a place in life. Our Lord said, *'the first shall be last, and the last first.'* He also said, *'In as much as ye hath done it to one of the least of my brethren, ye hath done it unto me.'*

Another expense these days was taking the children to and from school with cars bringing youngsters short distances which they could easily have walked. This led to traffic chaos outside the school twice a day. A very large bus picked the children up and took them to the comprehensive at Tregony each day making equal chaos there. The cost of sending a child to that school was also large with things they must have enormous compared to my days at Veryan. Playgroups were emerging with Veryan being rather slow but getting there in the end. Numbers at Veryan School were growing and in somebodies wisdom an extra class was thought necessary. There were 75 pupils at the time with numbers projected to rise. In my day there were 115 in the same space and we managed alright. The head teacher was Mrs Surridge when the extension was opened in July 1998. Having been invited I attended the opening, and was amazed how the school had changed. The children sat at tables instead of desks; there was a library and office, with a telephone which had been in use for years. I recall ringing the school in 1992 and being told, 'I'll put you through,' it was the school secretary, which also made me smile. She was just one sign of how red tape and rules had changed since I was there. The children have to have so many square feet each I was told when I queried the need for a new room. I admit to saying nonsense under my breath.

However it gave me the chance to talk with one or two governors concerning the school reunion I was considering for the next year. To my surprise they were quite happy with the idea so long as I had one of them on my committee. The committee was formed and we decided to have the event during May 1999. It was finally pencilled in for May 1st for which plans went ahead. I must say at this juncture how very helpful everyone at the school were. It was to be the very first such event at the school which is my reason for including so much on the subject. Parking was arranged at the social club with transport to bring people from it to the school. The P.F.A. very kindly took charge of the refreshments, and two cakes were made. We were blessed with fine weather on what turned out to be a wonderful day. Some 150 former pupils and teachers attended and signed the visitor's book we bought for the day. Some eight teachers were actually present including Miss Walker, now Mrs Sayell, who had taught me some fifty-four years before. A few of the many evacuees who attended the school in the forties were also present. I was very proud as I rose to speak having watched Mrs Unsworth cut the cake. In his reply, the vicar, standing in for Mrs Surridge (the head teacher who was unwell) said, how very different school was now compared to what I'd described. The one small blot on my happy day was the memory of teachers who had so influenced me for good that were no longer with us. The same went for pupils, especially Peter Harris, who's idea the whole thing had been. One of the kindest souls I have ever known – I still miss his lovely smile. Many who attended chose to eat the cake with no icing made by the school cook. The remainder of the iced one, made by Mrs Mary Symons, was brought to me and slices were sent to ex-pupils, unable to attend through sickness. So on the following Monday morning I went to the school in order to thank her. Imagine my surprise when at 9 a.m. she hadn't yet put in an appearance. Good God, I thought, Mrs Moses used to begin at half past seven. Another thing that's changed, I thought, feeling a bit cross.

At our two surgeries (a new one had been built at Tregony), staff came and went, there were so many I couldn't keep pace. The one at Portscatho had been extended with a waiting room now containing twenty chairs. A physiotherapist was now part of the team along with four or five doctors and God knows how many nurses. There were something like nine receptionists, many part-time, with a dispenser dishing out thousands of pills. A visit to the place often takes me back to the days before the health service when folk couldn't afford to see a doctor. I often think how times have changed the health service, which has been so good to me, often it reminds me of that song Louie Armstrong used to sing, 'And I think to myself what a wonderful world.' Alison Rawling and others had been fundraising for liver research for some time and in July 1990 Anna had a transplant.

Early in the decade I took a walk to Trewartha Chapel. It was in a terrible state, a board giving notice of its impending sale stood nearby. It was a long time before I ventured up there again. Memories came flooding back of how my parents had met here, married within its walls and brought me here to be christened. Of the wonderful folk who had so influenced my life, as the Chapel became part of my growing up. Sometimes in my dreams I am back in that Chapel, praying for our boys away at war, or bidding for something at the Harvest sale. The Christian faith instilled in me there has been the cornerstone of everything I have and am.

Canon Geach left Veryan after a long spell, during which he had become loved and respected. When he was ill some years later, many who never went near the church were concerned about him. He visited my father soon after mum died, which I will never forget, and was proud to see him bury both my parents. During his time the bells went to Loughborough and the organ was repaired. Mr Fred Reynolds, who did much in the village, passed away in 1991 and Mrs Margery Truscott took his place as Church Warden. We had a period without a vicar following Canon Geach's departure, about eighteen months, before another arrived. He came for five years, but would leave again before the time was up. While here he attempted to bring more young people into the church, which some of the older members didn't like. An attempt was also made to get a Sunday School going but it didn't work. The number of dwellings in the village had tripled, while at the same time places of worship were struggling.

One day I sat and pondered how Sunday had changed during my lifetime. When a boy, no work but what was absolutely necessary was carried out on the farm. Food for the cattle tied up indoors was often prepared the day before. The horses that worked so hard all week had a day of rest. Almost everyone had the day off work when they attended a place of worship. It was the only place one could go as no other events took place on that day. Most of us had our best clothes, or Sunday clothes as they were often known. Harvest festivals were for places of worship only we did have one at school. These days Sunday is no different from any other day, with tractors on the roads and many functions of note reserved for that day. Many shops are open – it's said because families have no other day to go shopping. Most folk only work five days a week now, being free on one weekday, so why can't they do the shopping then. I know from experience while one stays open people will come. Some make a habit of coming at the last minute. If shops were open twenty-four hours a day someone would come. This is all very fine for big stores who have staff but I still think it unnecessary.

In the forties many men worked a six day week, their wives did the shopping in the area where they lived. Shops opened Monday to Saturday and were run by their owners with some staff. I'm old fashioned enough to think that was right. Everything has to be big these days, but I must get off my high horse.

The Royal British Legion had only about six members now, which was inevitable given the length of time since the second war. Younger men who had done National Service were eligible but didn't appear interested. Towards the end of the century the branch was disbanded and the hall put up for sale. It would continue but under different management. It was purchased at auction by a local resident who in a most generous gesture gave it to the village. A public meeting was called to elect a committee who would run the place now to be called the Parish Hall. They started work immediately with functions being held to raise funds.

A local resident had an idea to put a footpath between the Green and Veryan. It would be on land farmed by the late Mr Melville Rundle and hopefully funded by Millenium money, soon to be available. The land was to be given and the whole scheme was put before the parish council. Being a person with poor sight and no car I was very much in favour and wrote to the Council saying as much. The scheme would also involve putting new wooden bridges over the water garden as it had been when it was put there in 1930.

The great royal tragedy nationally came on the last day of August 1997 when the much-loved Princess of Wales was killed in France. Not everybody's idea of an ideal person – she most certainly was mine. And the great outpouring of public emotion during the week that followed would suggest that many of the British people shared my view. That week culminating in her funeral the following Saturday: will remain with me as long as I live. Elton Johns rendering of *Candle in the Wind* had me close to tears. The response to her death from people in many countries showed very clearly how popular she had become. Much has been written about her – since most of it would have been better left unsaid. My final words on the subject are, 'I would have loved her to have been our Queen.' Why? Because she was different from the other royals.

On my retirement I began going for long walks! These were brought about by the need to keep fit and a longing to walk again where I had often gone as a boy. The ones chosen were Carbence Lane and the beach. The former I'd walked with my dad when I accompanied him for a day at my aunts, this when he worked at Treburthes. Early in my working life I went there to cut pea and bean sticks. One day I sat down for a while and nodded off. In a kind of dream I saw dad coming across the field with Madam my uncle's horse. For a few seconds it seemed very real, how I wished it could have been but time has moved on.

Walking to Carne beach took me past Trewartha where I'd both gone to Chapel and worked the land for many years. The former had closed and someone else had my field.

At the beach much had changed with notices concerning dogs and powerboats on display. I would sit on one of two wooden seats and remember. Walking up the steep hill on my way home tired me more these days. I didn't meet many people walking but when I met someone it struck me how much better off they all looked. Which I guess it's why fewer walk – most people can afford a car, or cars, something thought impossible fifty years ago. When I was a boy few people had more than two outfits – working clothes and those worn on Sundays.

Chapter Seven

A NEW CENTURY

The 21st century opened with a mass photograph taken at Carne Beacon, in which many of the villagers took part.

The garage built by Mr Morse has now gone replaced by a large bungalow lived in by his son. Very near the decades end the building that once housed Mr Elliott's lorries was partly taken down and rebuilt. Eight houses changed hands at Veryan Green in sixteen months during 2008-9 for ridiculous sums. The farm at Trewartha which Mr Rundle farmed for most of my life was also sold. Some of it will be let out to contractors for vegetable growing.

Throughout the early years of the new century the parish hall went from strength to strength. Much voluntary labour was involved and the committee changed somewhat. New heating was installed, the kitchen improved and an extension added. There was also a small car parking area. A host of functions were held in it and in one particular year bookings exceeded the number of days in a year. It's wonderful to see the place doing so well and as a lifelong parishioner there's nobody more grateful to the people who have worked so hard to make it successful. However knowing its history and why it was built it will always be for me The Royal British Legion Hall. A monument to Veryan people who fought and died in two world wars. They gave their lives that we might have freedom.

On the 13th and 14th of August 2005, the W.I. put on a display to celebrate 60 years since the Second World War ended. Many items from that era were on display including some cars. I wondered how the halls popularity would affect the clubhouse. When it started the legion was on the wane and continued to do so. Many events moved there amid rumblings of it being less central. A new century was to bring change with more returning to be waning. Others shared my feelings as stories of fights etc grew. Eight years into the century the bar was closed, and a working party set up. Early in 2009 questionnaires were distributed, and in March of that year a new chairman and trustees were elected to the hall which is more central. A group was set up to seek new ways of making the club viable. I hope they do, for I hate anything to fail in Veryan. Work concerning the water garden was completed. The main change being new wooden bridges as when it was first made. These had been replaced by stone ones in the late fifties. An enclosed case on legs containing photographs was erected near one of these bridges.

The footpath, to be known as Rundles Walk, caused great controversy, splitting the Parish Council. It was brought to a head at a meeting in April 2000 when the Parish Council voted against the scheme and one member resigned after an unsavoury meeting which I don't consider worth writing about. The path was opened after a time and my journey to the Post Office was much safer. I made no secret of my support for it and have since heard many locals and tourists sing it praises. They like the beautiful scenery and being close to the animals and also point out the safety factor. A second path was made from the top of Veryan down to the beach.

While on the subject of safety one seldom sees a child walking to or from school these days. They mostly come by car, which in turn makes it chaotic outside the school when they come and go. This is especially bad when a big funeral is taking place. The church opened a small parking area which helps but isn't nearly big enough. I am well aware it wouldn't be safe for children to walk to school as they once did with so much traffic, however, I cannot see why parents living within walking distance couldn't walk with them instead of cluttering the place with so many cars. I can honestly say I've seen them when the children live less than four hundred yards away. There have been calls for a parking area at Veryan Green since the mid eighties, but cars still line the road through the village by night and day.

Parc Behan was sold by the National Trust and became a private residence once more.

Tim George set up in business as a joiner in the garage next to Rockers Retreat. His fine workmanship soon got him a good reputation. Rickard Hancock and his wife, continued to build a good business at Melinsey Mill. A couple named Taylor arrived at the Roseland Stores. They were the first Cornish people to run it for 54 years. Grannies Attic is now run by Mrs Gray as an antique shop. The new owners of Hillside (to whom it belongs) have had work done on it.

Our milkman retired to be followed by a large dairy from miles away. A new butcher began coming round, named Radmore; he is a farmer's son. In 2009 eight different people, male and female, delivered our post until it was combined with Portloe and delivered by van.

The Channon's whose father had started way back in 1946 retired. When their mother passed away it was the end of the generation who were adults when I was a boy. The number of locals left in Veryan had dwindled with just three who had been here longer than myself. Many had lived in the parish as long but not the village. There were more people self-employed as many, on losing their job, set up as gardeners etc.

Veryan School, at the close of the decade, had eighty pupils. Mr Welsh who was head for much of it has gone; he was the first male head for some nineteen years. Followed by a lady supply head in the autumn of 2008, a permanent female then took over. Her name is Mrs Latham and she works closely with the church where the pupils go for assembly once a week. They also rehearse for and give end of term concerts etc. Our present vicar, Mr Robbins, attended Veryan School as a boy and his family have links with the parish going back many years.

Very late in the decade Mrs Sayell (Miss Walker) passed away. The Margaret Walker Cup, to be presented each year is a permanent memorial to her time there.

I can't mention every death in the village during this decade, it wouldn't be possible, but will say a few words about Mrs Hampshire, a popular lady, who worked tirelessly raising money for a liver charity. This leads on to the church where a vast amount of money was raised to restore the windows, some of which won't be completed this decade. The parish had two vicars; Mr Buddon, and later Mr Robbins, the latter assisted by Mr Williams. Mrs Truscott was joined as churchwarden by Mr Smith, who were followed by Mr Elliott and Mrs Craven. At the time of writing the organist is Mrs Goldie.

The much liked Dr Price retired to be replaced by a lady, Dr Jervis. The email system was introduced as a way of ordering repeat prescriptions. This proved a godsend to me and probably others with poor sight. I can no longer keep up with the number of staff at the two surgeries, but have nothing but praise for them all. My support though wasn't much in evidence when I sent them an unstamped Christmas card one year. Early in 2010 I received a letter saying Dr Jervis was retiring at the end of March. As with Dr Price before her, she had been more like a friend than a Doctor.

Early in the decade the W.I. decided to get rid of the wooden structure they had used for over fifty years and hold their meetings in the parish hall instead. During August in 2005 and 2008 they organised exhibitions to mark first the 60th anniversary of the Second World War ending and second ninety years of the W.I. being founded. A great many people attended them both.

Sport seems popular still at the wonderful facilities the sports centre provides, sadly there are few local boys wanting to play cricket, players come from outside to make up a team. While on the subject of play, as the decade draws to a close work has begun to turn the Maurlonder into a super play area for the children of Veryan. A new entrance has been made into the school near the parish hall.

As I write in early January 2010 the population of Veryan Green must be at an all time low. There are 23 properties empty for different reasons and about 75 people actually living here. I doubt if there have ever been less throughout my lifetime. When my story began at the start of 1940, before any evacuees came, 90 people lived in the 39 dwellings – well over 2 in each. It's now with sixty-three dwellings just over one. I compare Veryan Green, as I know it better, while Veryan itself has grown so much comparison is well nigh impossible. The Green had nearly one working person per house, it's now one per nine houses.

The number of empty properties and decline in working people show clearly how this end of the village has altered in seven decades. With over 175 dwelling in Veryan itself the proportion of those empty is far less, with the ratio of people in work higher.

After much thought my conclusions are; the biggest change is in the amount of luxury goods most of us now own. Let's look at things that were either classed as such, or didn't exist in the forties. Few owned a car or telephone and many electrical goods hadn't been invented. Bathrooms were few as was an indoor toilet. Most of us had a radio by the decades end. All these things are now in most homes whether a member of the household works or not. On top of those mentioned a wide array of electrical goods can be found in many homes.

A great many people have come to live in our village during my lifetime. A high percentage of them have only remained for a while, before returning to be nearer their families. A few have chosen to end their days here and some are buried in Veryan churchyard. Some don't like the incomers but most of our organisations couldn't keep going without them.

Most of the newcomers I welcome for I feel we should be willing to share our lovely village and our county for that matter. If I went to live in another place I wouldn't want folk to be against me because I wasn't one of them. Having thus said nothing would please me more than to see more Cornish in Veryan again.

Despite all the changes, life in the village I love so much goes forward. New born babies take the place of those that have been here all my life and so it will go on. To end, what will probably be my last offering, I will close with the lines which ended my first:

Here in the countries heart
Where the grass is green
Life is the same sweet life
As it ere hath been.

ALSO AVAILABLE FROM PALORES PUBLICATIONS

TREMANYON – *A Shadow Falls* – by Carol Symons

After a fire destroys the house on the manor of Tremayne, Richard Tremayne and his family return from London to Cornwall where, on the site of the ruins on the beautiful Rhosinnis Peninsular, he undertakes the building of a Georgian Manor House, Tremanyon.

Local young woman, Ginifur Retallick. is employed as a maid for his wife Annabelle and their two young daughters. Annabelle is determined to give Richard a son but, although she has given birth to two healthy children, the third child is 'still born' – casting a 'shadow' over the peninsular.

At the request of William Pitt and Lord Falmouth, Richard sails to the New World at the beginning of the French and Indian War; during the period when the English, Irish and Scots settlers were living with the constant danger of attack and their homesteads burned to the ground.

Meanwhile, in the two years Richard is absent from Cornwall, many things are changing at Tremanyon. But 'Old Betsy', the White Witch who lives on the edge of the village, promises that the shadow will be lifted.

ISBN 978-906845-21-6   Price: £7.95

DRECKLY – *A Collection of Possibilities* – by Les Merton

A collection of futuristic writing which at times digs into the bedrock of Cornwall and its legends.

Men Scryfa, The Mermaid of Zennor, Men-an-Tol, Dozmary Pool, The Cheesewring and many other subjects are given a speculative treatment.

ISBN 978-1-906845-24-7   Price: £6.00